Holy Death
Bible

© First Edition in Spanish, Guerrero Editores, México 1995
© 1st Edition in Spanish USA Calli Casa Editorial 2014
2a Edition in Spanish, revised, USA, Calli Casa Editorial 2021
1st. Edition in English, USA, Yhacar Trust, 2022

General Supervision: Bernabé Pérez
Cover Illustration: Mehmet Can Doğan (fiverr.com/mecandon)
www.2GoodLuck.com
jbooks909@gmail.com, Lake Elsinore, CA 92530

Cult of Death

Mexican culture has maintained a close and even reverent relationship with Death since its conception. As time went by, this relationship became a cult that has spread to many corners and civilizations of ancient Mexico, including the Mayans, Zapotecs, Mixtecs, Totonacs, and, of course, the Mexica or Aztecs.

As part of their beliefs, the Mexica maintained the cult of the two gods, Mictlantecuhtli and Mictecacihuatl, who were considered to be "lord" and "lady" of darkness and Death. Not only were they entrusted with the deceased, but they were also invoked to obtain other favors.

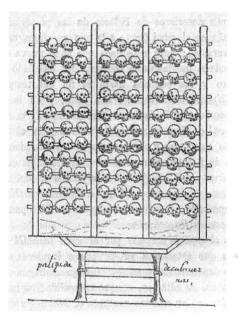

Tzompantli was one of the practices of these cultures, which could be translated as "wall of skulls". These rows of skulls were placed one on top of the other, showcasing the skulls of those dead in sacrifices to the gods. It is also believed that there were also exhibited the skulls of enemies killed in war campaigns. (Figure taken from the Durán Codex. Commons.Wikimedia.org ID: 356895).

The Spanish colonization managed to decrease the cult of Death, but not to eradicate it completely. It remained latent until the 19th century when it took place an organic resurgence in its devotion. It was born from the barrios through people who secretly worshiped

Santa Muerte (Holy Death). These worshippers suddenly began to take to the streets with images of skulls, dressed in robes of different colors, which caused the followers to discover that they were not alone, therefore joining the "movement".

In the pre-Hispanic era, it is said that its official day is November 1st, Day of the "Little Dead" and November 2nd, the official Day of the Dead or All Soul's Day.

During those days, an altar full of offerings and multicolored candles was placed, as the faithful followers prostrated themselves around it, expressing repentance and devotion to their dead and to Death itself.

The offering was placed under the protection of Coatlicue and Mictlantecuhtli, deities of the Earth and the Underworld, respectively. These deities of the pre-Hispanic times were similar to saints in the Catholic religion.

Although the resurgence of the contemporary cult of the image emerged around 1965, historians trace the belief and devotion to Death back many years.

"It is very difficult to fix an exact date of the emergence of the cult. It is most likely that it a product of the fusion of the pre-Hispanic and European cultures of Death at the time of the Colony, which has remained hidden for several centuries and it is coming to light in recent years", the scholars of this cult claim.

The Catholic Church condemns this veneration and considers it to be "sinful", but many people associate this practice with the Church. Meanwhile, most of the followers do not seem to be interested in the contradiction between their religion and their cult of Death.

For this reason, they organize rituals similar to Christian ones, which include processions and prayers in order to repay their favors.

Many followers even make their own altars in their home, office, or business to feel protected by the Holy Death. The altar usually consists of a statue whose measurements range from 5 centimeters (2 inches) to 2 meters (just over two yards). It is surrounded by different offerings, like floral arrangements, fruits, incenses, wines, coins, candies, beer, and candy, next to candles that vary in color depending on the subject of the request.

Cigars, which must be constantly lit, a piece of bread, water, and salt are considered essential.

People come to ask for miracles or favors related to love, health, work, and protection.

Supporters often identify themselves with a pendant or scapular with her image on it, while others choose to have her figure tattooed on their skin.

Those who come to her altar venerate her as if she were a Catholic saint, making the sing of the cross and praying to her so their requests are fulfilled.

At the beginning of the 21st century, the attachment to this belief ceased to be clandestine and spread to the United States due to the immigration of its disciples. They claim to have been safe on their journey thanks to their "Santa Muerte" by carrying her image in their clothing to maintain her continued protection.

Her followers say they have crossed the border "safe and sound" thanks to her influence.

Adoration of Santa Muerte

This cult, which continues growing because of its great strength, is linked to the tradition of the Day of the Dead. Its historical roots from both pre-Hispanic and colonial times also fit very well with contemporary Mexico.

The sculpture of the Holy Death -also known as the Lady of Shadows, White Lady, Black Lady, Holy Girl, Grim Reaper, La Flaca (The Skinny One), La Hermana Blanca (The White Sister), La Niña Bonita (The Pretty Girl)- is becoming more and more popular.

It has the traditional figure of the Day of the Dead skull and is dressed in costumes of different colors, each one with a special meaning.

Santa Muerte has a scythe, a scale, and it is holding the world in her hands. She can be adorned with pearl, gold, and silver bracelets embedded with precious stones as offerings. These are hanged by the faithful when they want to thank her for a miracle or favor received.

During the feast of Santa Muerte is on November 2nd, also known as the Day of the Dead, her followers dress in white at night and dedicate a rosary to her. On the first day of each month, nightly rosaries take place to bless the images carried by followers on statues, scapulars, medals, boxes, tattoos, and so on.

Note: Some followers claim that the official day of worship is August 15. Many celebrate both dates.

Those who visit her altar pay homage to her with the same devotion as they do to Christ, the saints, and the virgins. They make the sign of the cross, pray, ask for favors, and make offerings.

Many have the false notion that Santa Muerte collects the favors received, but some others say this is not the case. When you receive a favor from her, you only have to do a favor to someone else in gratitude. In other words, according to this belief, "love is repaid with love." If you receive a good, you must pass it on to the next person to be on good terms with Santa Muerte.

Another misconception is that Santa Muerte only helps drug traffickers in criminal matters. While it is true that many outlaws have been arrested carrying ostentatious gold images of Santa Muerte, this does not imply that this cult is exclusive to them. Because of this mistaken belief, some prisons in California prohibit inmates from receiving books about Santa Muerte, thinking that it is a way to "lure" readers into committing new criminal acts. Serious mistake. Those who prohibit prisoners from receiving these books do not speak Spanish and do not understand this religious cult that is spreading from the United States, crossing all over Mexico up to Guatemala, being adopted by all kinds of people.

According to some cult leaders, it is very possible that a formal petition may be initiated in the United States to recognize the cult as a religion, allowing them to acquire the same rights to freedom and respect that other religions enjoy in the United States.

Christian Devotion?

The spread of the cult of Santa Muerte in Mexico has caused its followers to stop hiding their fervor to start placing altars in the street so that anyone who requires her help can invoke her.

In 2000, the Mexican-American Traditionalist Catholic Church (IS-CAT), requested the formal registration of this church before the Secretary of the Interior in Mexico (SEGOB), without mentioning its relationship with the cult of Santa Muerte. The registration was granted in 2003. Since that year, the church began to display the image of Santa Muerte as its central figure of worship.

In 2005, the General Directorate of Religious Associations filed a complaint with SEGOB, after which the ISCAT permit was withdrawn.

The cult leaders reapplied to SEGOB for registration in 2006, which has encountered opposition and, since then, it has been in a legal process full of advances and setbacks.

Despite all conflicts over legal recognition of the movement as a church, the popular cult has continued to grow in Mexico and even to transcend borders.

Its followers, who have stopped hiding their beliefs, have left the rooms where they kept hidden altars to show up in ceremonies in squares, meeting centers, parks, and other public places. Now, the faithful even wear pendants on their wrists and necklaces to publicly display their faith in Santa Muerte.

Movies have been made, songs of various genres have been composed, books have been written, and perfumes, oils, statues, amulets, soaps, jewelry, and many other items have been created for her followers to identify with.

And the cult of Santa Muerte has advanced relentlessly on both sides of the Mexican border.

Statue of Our Señora Muerte

Here you will find the colors of Santa Muerte's robes and their meanings when making an altar for her. These colors can be present in her clothes or you can buy a statue in the color of your choice, changing the color of the tablecloth on which the statue is placed as the intention of the rituals or prayers change.

Colors and purposes:

Blue

The color of understanding and concentration. It can help students who need to graduate with a degree or pass an exam, as well as people who have creative talents, such as writers, illustrators, or musicians.

White

The color white represents purification, cleansing, peace, harmony, and light. It is used for when you need to be in that positive vibration.

Gold

As the name implies, it is the color of gold. It is used to attract money, prosperity, and luxury. It serves to pave the way to bright days of economic well-being.

Purple

The color of transmutation. It is used to change negatives into positives, to wish for the positive in a situation to manifest itself, and to protect against negative vibrations, including those related to health.

Orange

The color of protection for health. It is used to remove all types of natural diseases, created or caused.

Black

The color of protection. We can use it to say goodbye to a loved one who is no longer with us, so that they may go in peace. Or it is also used to protect us from dangers lurking at night or in the dark, and to protect us from people with bad vibes or negative situations.

Red

This color is essential for any ritual related to love, passion, and sexual integration of the couple. To unite two people who have separated or who barely met, with whom one wishes to consolidate love.

Pink

This color helps in everything related to love, either family, friendship, or couple love. It is the love that serves, that smiles, that has goodwill, and that builds.

Ritual of consecration:

What you will need:

Rose oil or water,

Rue oil,

Water and salt,

Censer with frankincense, myrrh, or benzoin tears,

Bee honey,

Rose or red carnation petals,

A container to wash your image,

A little bit of vodka,

A white candle.

Directions:

It is recommended to do it on Saturday, as this day has positive energy for rituals of religious nature.

1. The statue of Santa Muerte is washed in salted water. As the image is being washed, cleaning all road dust and mentally blessing it, we have to thank her for coming into our lives. It is washed respectfully and slowly.

2. Throw away the water in which the image was washed. Afterward, the image is left to dry, preferably in the sun.

3. Put clean water in a container and add the rose petals, a few drops of rue oil, a few drops of rose oil or rose water, a drop of honey, and a little bit of vodka.

4. The statue is placed in the designated place on the altar and the white candle is lit, as well as the censer with the chosen incense.

5. The smoke should be spread all over the house, especially the altar area (it may be necessary to add more incense).

6. As we go walk the house with the incense, the candle and the statue of Santa Muerte to welcome her home, we raise our thoughts

and ask our entity to come and enter the statue at that moment. That way, she can enter the statue whenever we call her.

7. We repeat: "Santa Muerte, I am calling you to come to this place, take this statue and give it life... Hail Santa Muerte."

8. Once we show Santa Muerte each room of the house and we ask her to bless it, she is returned to the altar. We say: "This is the place where you will be and where we will honor you. Hail Santa Muerte."

The place where the altar was built will be a place of meditation and prayer for us, so we must keep it clean and in harmony.

Santa Muerte usually brings a world, a scythe, and a scale. She may also bring an owl and other items. If she does not bring them all, we can add them to the altar so that she has all her elements.

Elements that accompany Santa Muerte

Scale:

Mystical symbol of justice. It represents equity. It means that all aspects of a situation will always be considered in order to be totally fair when giving a sentence or making a decision.

It symbolizes that justice is impartial, as it can be seen in its most common form, with two hanging plates symmetrically arranged.

On the whole, it helps us to have stability, peace, firmness, and security.

Owl:

The owl represents being comfortable with our own shadow. Freedom, visual acuity. The link between the spiritual world and the earthly plane. Messenger of secrets and omens. Lunar magic, secrecy, seeing behind the masks, shape-shifting. It is silence and swift movement, stealth.

As a bird that moves in the dark, it helps us, to get out of any situation we may have, no matter how confused and blind we may be by it.

This bird is related to wisdom and is the messenger of Santa Muerte.

Lantern:

It represents the light that radiates and shows us with clarity the path and the decisions we must make in our lives. A symbol of the spirit and its intelligence.

The perpetual flame of its lamp represents the light that cannot be extinguished: the light of spirit. The light that illuminates the darkness and casts it out, that takes us out of ignorance and shows us the truth.

It is spiritual clarity, peace, and harmony.

It is the symbol of intelligence and spirit. Its light shows us the clarity of the path and the decisions we make throughout our lives.

Scythe:

It cuts off bad energies, bad influences, evil matters. When used in cultivation, it is a tool that allows us to reap what we have sown.

A symbol of new hope and prosperity.

World:

Speaking generally, "having the world in your hands" represents confidence, success, conquest, independence, and leadership. A symbol of power to which we should aspire.

Hourglass:

The hourglass is relentless in measuring time. Like Cronus, the Greek god of time, it is in charge of making us see that the days, — either if we take advantage of them or if we lose them—, are gone and do not return.

Symbol that warns us to take care of our time to make the most of it. We do not know how many days we have left, so the days that pass in our lives must count for something positive.

Establishing goals and completing them little by little each day until they are achieved.

... After this experience Rosario did not want to continue working in the warehouse. She looked for another job. After a few days she felt more serene. She then returned to look for the policewoman to thank her for her timely. She came to the Police Station and asked all her employees about her. They all gave her the same answer: "No female police officers worked there. For a long time they had only hired male police officers".

She insisted that it was a female police officer who had rescued her. "There are no women here," the employees repeated, already annoyed at her insistence.

She got out of there. And she realized something. She remembered that she had invoked the Santa Muerte in the supreme instant of her terrifying experience. At that moment she put her hand on the image that she was carrying around her neck. She began to caress her figure. Little crystalline pearls rolled down her cheeks. Without waiting any longer, she went straight to the sanctuary of the Santa Muerte. She now knew exactly who she should thank for having been saved ..."

Fragment of the story: "La Bodega", taken from the book
"Testimonies of the Blessed Holy Death",
by Juan Ambrosio and Laila Pita

Altars

Against alcoholism:

What you will need:

1 dozen flowers (of the kind that you prefer),
1 vase of your choosing,
1 image of Santa Muerte,
1 white tablecloth,
1 prayer card of Santa Muerte or a picture,
1 black ink pen,
1 glass of wine of the alcoholic patient's choice,
1 white or pink candle,
1/2 meter of purple ribbon.

Directions:

1. Find a suitable place to set up your altar.

2. Place the tablecloth and the image of Santa Muerte on top of it.

3. Write down the name of the patient three times on the prayer card or the picture. Wrap the paper completely with the purple ribbon.

4. Place the wrapped prayer card next to the wine glass, next to your Santa Muerte.

5. Turn on the candle. Repeat three times the sick person's name. Make your request to Santa Muerte immediately, asking to remove this vice from (say the name of the sick person) or whatever you want to ask for this person. Let the candle burn out in its entirety.

6. Place the vase with the chosen flowers on the altar.

7. Lastly, pour the wine down the drain. From time to time, you have to place a new wine next to the image of Santa Muerte, repeating the name and making the request again. Do so until you start seeing results.

Against Bad Luck:

What you will need:

1 dollar bill,

1 glass of brandy,

1 glass of cane molasses or honey,

1 bottle of Road Opener oil,

1 statue of Santa Muerte,

1 yellow tablecloth,

1 piece of golden thread,

1 piece of Santeria stick "Yo puedo más que tú" (I can do more than you)

1 jet stone,

1 handful of toasted corn,

1 shelf,

1 candle of choice,

12 small coins,

2 cigars,

6 white carnations.

Directions:

1. Find a suitable place to set up your altar.

2. Add the shelf and put your tablecloth on it.

3. Clean your statue of Santa Muerte thoroughly with Road Opener oil and place it in the middle of the shelf.

4. Place the candle in front of her as you say the following pray:

"O Miraculous Santísima Muerte (Holiest Death), I come prostrate before you to ask and beg you to cover this house with your holy hand so that jinxes and curses, envy and hatred may never touch it. In this your home, O my Lady, you are welcome! I leave you all my faith, my thoughts, and my deeds on your altar and, in your honor, I give you this light and this money so that neither I nor my people ever lack. Thank you, Lady, for the favors received. Amen".

5. Proceed to place the brandy, carnations and cane molasses or honey.

6. Next, spread the dollar bill and place the jet stone on top of it, as

well as the coins and the piece of stick.

7. Wrap it all up. Tie it with the golden thread, and as you are doing it, focus and ask for you to do well in any area, that nothing may be difficult for you, and that it may open the roads there are and are yet to be.

8. Proceed to place the wrapper on the plate next to the corn.

9. Lastly, light the two cigars and leave them burning on a plate in front of the altar. Watch until they are consumed and then throw the ash in a garden and the cigarette butts in the trash.

For blessing of jobs or projects:

What you will need:
1 dollar bill,
1 glass of sherry,
1 bottle of Santa Muerte perfume,
1 statue of Santa Muerte,
1 used key,
1 white tablecloth,
1 meter of ribbon,
1 piece of Unblocking Santeria stick,
1 piece of Kraft paper,
1 plate, preferably earthenware,
1 handful of sunflower seeds,
1 cigar,
1 shelf,
1 Steady Job candle,
3 candies,
3 coins,
6 red carnations.

Directions:

1. Find a suitable place for the shelf.

2. Place the tablecloth on the shelf and put the statue of Santa Muerte in the middle of the shelf.

3. Clean your statue with perfume and place the candle in front of Santa Muerte. Light the candle and say the following prayer:

"O Santísima Muerte, bless this candle so that it may illuminate my path. May the projects I have, been granted to me without any difficulty. I come to you, prostrated, so that you may fulfill my needs. May the eyes of others see me with goodwill and may their trust be placed in me. Thank you, my Lady, for the favors received."

4. Proceed to write on a piece of Kraft paper your full name and the name of the person who can help you find a job, your future boss, the name of the company you want to join, or the type of job you are looking to find.

5. Then, place the coins, the piece of stick, the key, and the dollar bill on the piece of paper. Wrap it all up and tie it with ribbon.

6. Next, place some sunflower seeds on a plate, preferably an earthenware plate, and place the wrapped paper on top of them.

7. Light your cigar and leave it next to your Santa Muerte.

8. Once your wish has been granted, place a small offering on top of it, either a candle, a cigar, a wine bottle, or flowers of your choice.

9. You should leave the wrapped paper there for some time. If a family member has a similar problem, you must do the same work that you did for yourself.

10. Regarding the maintenance of your altar, this will depend on you. You should keep it clean and always full of light to obtain good results.

For good fortune in business:

What you will need:

1 dollar bill,
1 beer,
1 statue of Santa Muerte,
1 yellow tablecloth,
1 piece of Road Opener Santeria stick,
1 piece of tortilla,
1 bottle of Santa Muerte perfume,
1 jet stone,
1 magnet stone,
1 stone from the entrance of the business (small),
1 plate, preferably earthenware,
1 cigar,
1 shelf,
1 piece of chocolate,
1 Good Luck, Road Opener and/or Wealth & Prosperity candle,
12 coins,
3 red roses.

Directions:

1. Secure your shelf very well and place your tablecloth on it.

2. Place the statue of Santa Muerte in the middle of the altar.

3. Clean the statue of Santa Muerte with perfume very carefully.

4. Then, place your candle in front of it and light it with your right hand. Say the following prayer:

"O Santísima Muerte, I call you. I implore you for fortune, wealth and success to come to me. May this business never lack sustenance, harmony, and peace, so that you illuminate all the members of this business through this light. Please, remove envy and hatred from this space. Thank you, my Lady, for the favors received."

5. Place the flowers on one side of the statue and all the other ingredients on the other side, except for the coins, the dollar bill, the stones, the tortilla, and the Road Opener stick. These shall be placed on the plate, preferably earthenware, that will be placed next to San-

ta Muerte.

6. Regarding the cigar, it will be lit daily for one or two minutes.

7. Arrange all the elements on the altar according to your personal taste.

8. Remember that having an impeccably maintained altar of Santa Muerte will render your well-being, harmony, and success. A neglected altar will have very little results, and the maintenance of this altar will depend on you. Every time you want to ask for the prosperity of your business, you have to visualize yourself and the members of this business full of success, customers, and good fortune. Keep in mind that you must have faith and firmness in every ritual, always keep that vision in your mind and discard all doubts.

9. Flowers and light should always be present at your altar.

For a law firm:

What you will need:

1 scale,
1 stout beer,
1 coconut chunk,
1 statue of Santa Muerte,
1 green tablecloth,
1 alum stone,
1 magnet stone,
1 small plate, preferably earthenware,
1 white plate,
1 cigar,
1 Justice or Win Court Case Candle,
12 coins,
6 red carnations,
8 mint tablets,
A little bit of cane molasses or some honey.

Directions:

1. Find a safe place to set up your altar.

2. Secure the shelf and place the tablecloth on it. In the middle of it, place your Santa Muerte.

3. In front of your Santa Muerte, you will put the beer, the coconut, the molasses (on the plate, preferably earthenware).

4. Place the flowers on one side of the Santa Muerte statue and place the white plate with the stones, coins, and tablets on the other side.

5. Attach the scale to either one of Santa Muerte's hands and say the following:

"May the roads be opened politically, legally, occupationally, and administratively. May it be so".

6. Then, light your candle and pray the prayer that is written on the candle.

Remember that the petitions should be made with faith and firmness.

The molasses, coconut chunk and beer should be changed every week, while the flowers should be changed as often as necessary.

For spiritual development:

If you are developing in the spiritual plane and you want the Santa Muerte to be your guide, you should set up your altar for her to help you out with the works or doings that you want to carry out. Here, you will learn how to set up your altar for her miraculous image.

What you will need:

1 dollar bill,

1 glass of water (never should be missing),

1 glass of tequila,

1 statue of Santa Muerte,

1 used key,

1 white tablecloth,

1 piece of chocolate or cane molasses,

1 piece of Santeria stick each of Road Opener and Unblocking,

1 small stalk of maguey,

1 bottle of Santa Muerte perfume,

1 jet stone,

1 magnet stone,

1 plate, preferably earthenware,

1 handful of 12 different seeds,

1 cigar,

1 shelf,

1 pair of scissors,

1 Double Luck candle,

12 coins,

3 sewing needles,

3 red carnations,

3 red apples,

3 white roses.

Directions:

1. Assign a special place to the altar.

2. Place the shelf there.

3. Place the tablecloth on top of it.

4. Clean your statue of Santa Muerte with the perfume.

5. Then, place it in the middle of the shelf.

6. Light the candle and hold it in your hands. Say the following:

"O my Lady, welcome to this house of yours. Prostrate before you I come with my faith and my spiritual firmness so you may guide me towards the path of clairvoyance and grant me the faculty to help my fellow men. I ask you, Lady, to protect me from any adversity, natural or caused disease, and also from negative vibrations".

7. Arrange all the items on the list in the way you like the most. Change flowers and fruit as needed. Throw out the water and the tequila every three weeks and refill the glasses each with fresh water and fresh tequila.

For the student:

What you will need:

1 glass of red wine,
1 bottle of essence of Santa Muerte,
1 sheet of white paper,
1 sheet of Kraft paper,
1 statue of Santa Muerte,
1 piece of Santeria stick palo vencedor,
1 magnet stone,
1 plate, preferably earthenware,
1 shelf,
1 cup of coffee,
1 glass of water,
1 23rd Psalm or Wisdom candle,
3 needles,
3 yellow apples,
3 white roses,
Colored candies,
White tablecloth.

Directions:

1. Place the shelf in a place where it is secure and place the tablecloth on top.

2. Cleanse your statue of Santa Muerte with the perfume.

3. Then, place it in the middle of the shelf.

4. In front of your Santa Muerte, place your candle and say the prayer printed on it.

5. Write on a piece of Kraft paper the name of your teachers, the subjects, or the problem you want to solve.

6. Place it under your candle. Do this as many times as necessary.

7. Place one by one the glass of wine, the glass of water, the cup of coffee, the white roses, the candies, and the apples (the order and placement are up to personal taste).

8. Write your full name and the school where you are studying on a

white sheet of paper.

9. Place the white sheet of paper on the plate, preferably earthenware.

10. On top of it, put the magnet stone, the needles, and the piece of stick. This plate should always be on the altar, next to Santa Muerte. It will help you overcome any obstacle, no matter the difficulty of it. It depends on you how you take care of this altar, but it is suggested that you always keep it in very good clean condition.

11. Light the candle.

For the home:

What you will need:

1 pack of cigarettes,
1 new ashtray,
1 glass containing rum, tequila, or sherry (to taste),
1 Christ or Cross,
1 vase,
1 statue of Santa Muerte,
1 white tablecloth,
1 bunch of Dominican bananas,
1 piece of bread,
1 cup of water,
1 Peaceful Home candle,
3 red apples,
4 red carnations,
A little honey

Directions:

1. Find an appropriate place to set up your altar. Preferably, at the entrance of your house or in any room of it.

2. Place the shelf and put the tablecloth on it. Then, place your statue of Santa Muerte.

3. Next to it, place the glass of water and, behind it, put the cross or the Christ.

4. You should put the wine glass with the 3 apples on one side of the glass of water.

5. Later, start distributing the bread, bananas, honey, and cigarettes on the altar. It is suggested that two cigars are lit, one for you and the other for your Santa. Leave both cigars in an ashtray next to the Santa Muerte, taking precautions to make sure everything is safe. At the end of the ritual, put them out.

6. Proceed to put the vase with flowers next to Santa Muerte.

7. You should then light the candle. Pray an Our Father and the prayer that comes in your candle. At the end of the prayer, make your request very firmly.

For the restaurant:

What you will need:

1 pack of cigarettes,
1 ashtray,
1 glass cup with water,
1 spoonful of honey,
1 white vase,
1 white tablecloth,
1 white plate,
1 shelf (according to personal taste),
1 piece of white bread or whole-wheat bread,
1 statue of Santa Muerte,
1 Fast Money candle,
12 coins of your own, each one of a different denomination,
6 white carnations.

Directions:

1. Find a spot for your altar. Place your shelf and put the tablecloth on top of it. Then, set your Santa Muerte on the shelf.

2. In front of it, place the cup of water and repeat the following: "May prosperity and success come to this business. May there never be a shortage of money for everyone in this business. May our customers receive blessings through what they buy from us. So be it."

3. Next to the glass of water, place the coins and bread.

4. Next to Santa Muerte, place the vase with the carnations and put the honey on the white plate.

5. Light 2 cigars. One for you and the other for your Santa Muerte. Leave both cigars in an ashtray next to the Santa, taking precautions to make sure everything is safe. At the end of the ritual, put them out.

6. Light your candle on the altar and pray two Our Fathers and the prayer that comes with your candle.

Remember that the candle should only be lit when you are working. When closing your business, blow it off.

For the auto shop:

What you will need:

1 box of storax incense,

1 box of copal sticks,

1 ashtray,

1 chocolate,

1 cup of water,

1 glass of red wine,

1 statue of Santa Muerte,

1 yellow tablecloth,

1 medium-sized alum stone,

1 plate, preferably earthenware,

1 cigar,

1 bunch of Dominican bananas,

1 shelf (according to personal taste),

1 Prosperity candles,

3 coins of your own,

6 white carnations,

9 small tools (miniature toys).

Directions:

The statue of Santa Muerte that you are going to place on the altar is according to personal taste or the needs of the location.

1. Find an appropriate spot for the altar. Place the shelf on it and, on top of it, the tablecloth and the statue.

2. In front of Santa Muerte, set the plate, preferably earthenware. Inside of it, put the tools, the alum stone, the coins, and the chocolate.

3. Next to the plate, place the cup of water and the glass of wine.

4. Then, light your cigar. Smoke it repeatedly and apply the smoke to your Santa Muerte. Put the remaining in the ashtray next to the two glasses, making sure that it does not fall over.

5. Light your candle and pray the prayer printed on it. At the end of the prayer, make your request with faith and firmness. You should always visualize your business with great success and prosperity. The

candle should be lit when you are working, and blown off when you close your business.

6. With your candle, light two sticks of incense, one of copal and the other of storax or some other incense of your choice.

7. Set the carnations and bananas next to Santa Muerte.

8. Replace the ingredients of the altar as many times as necessary in order to keep it fresh and clean.

For the beauty salon:

What you will need:

1 box of sandalwood incense,
1 pack of cigarettes,
1 glass of brandy,
1 vase,
1 statue of Santa Muerte,
1 yellow tablecloth,
1 yellow apple,
1 red apple,
1 shelf (according to personal taste),
1 pack of cinnamon powder,
1 Fast Money or Don Juan del Dinero candle,
3 red roses,
7 coins,
A little honey

Directions:

1. Find an appropriate and safe spot to set up your altar. Place your shelf, the tablecloth, and your statue of Santa Muerte in the middle.

2. Next to Santa Muerte, put the vase with the roses. In front of it, place two cones or sticks of incense.

3. Then, proceed to put the apples and to sprinkle them with cinnamon. Next to them, place the glass of brandy and honey.

4. Light two cigars. Leave both cigars in an ashtray next to the statue of Santa Muerte, taking precautions to make sure everything is safe. At the end of the ritual, put them off.

5. Proceed to light your candle, pray an Our Father and the prayer printed on the candle. Once you have done this, place the seven coins next to the candle.

6. Once the candle has burned out, remove the coins and put them in your purse, wallet, or bag and spend them when needed, to make the money circulate.

For the grocery store:

What you will need:

1 box of incense, preferably jasmine,
1 pack of cigarettes,
1 ashtray,
1 cup of water,
1 cross or Christ of any material,
1 statue of Santa Muerte,
1 yellow tablecloth,
1 magnet stone,
1 shelf,
1 glass of brandy,
1 Wealth and Prosperity or Road Opener candle,
3 needles,
3 red roses,
A little honey

Directions:

1. Find an appropriate and safe spot to set up your altar.

2. Place your shelf and, on top of it, the tablecloth. Put your statue of Santa Muerte in the middle of it.

3. In front of the statue, you should put the ashtray with the magnet stone inside of it, as well as the needles and the cross or the Christ.

4. Next to Santa Muerte, put the vase with red roses and honey and brandy next to them.

5. Light two incense sticks and let them burn next to the statue.

6. Light two cigars. Leave both cigars in an ashtray next to the Santa Muerte, taking precautions to make sure everything is safe. At the end of the ritual, put them off.

7. Lastly, light the candle and pray the prayer printed on it.

Remember you should always visualize your business with great success and financial prosperity while doing this. You should also visualize your customers being happy and satisfied after having bought in your store. Change the materials you are using on your altar to Santa Muerte as many times as necessary to keep it clean and fresh.

For offices:

What you will need:

1 pack of cigarettes,

1 ashtray,

1 glass of sherry,

1 statue of Santa Muerte,

1 white tablecloth,

1 white plate,

1 white Santa Muerte candle,

12 coins,

3 white roses,

Colored candies,

Small scissors.

Directions:

1. Find the right spot to set up your altar. Place the shelf, the tablecloth, and the statue in the middle.

2. Put the roses next to Santa Muerte, and the plate with the scissors, the coins and the candies have to be placed in front of the flowers.

3. Next to the plate, you should put the glass of sherry.

4. Light two cigars. Leave both cigars in an ashtray next to the Santa, taking precautions to make sure everything is safe. At the end of the ritual, put them off.

5. Light your candle and pray the prayer printed on it. At the end of it, make your request with faith and firmness.

The candle should be on as you carry out your daily tasks, and you should only extinguish it when you finish working, before going home.

For businesses:

What you will need:

1 dollar bill,
1 box of myrrh incense cones,
1 coconut,
1 glass cup of water,
1 medium wooden or ocote cross,
1 statue of Santa Muerte,
1 yellow tablecloth,
1 piece of whole-wheat bread,
1 plate, preferably earthenware,
1 cigar,
1 shelf (according to personal taste),
1 Better Business candle,
3 red apples,
7 coins.

Directions:

1. Find an appropriate spot for your shelf, either the entrance of your business or near the place where you keep the money.

2. Upon placing the tablecloth on the shelf, proceed to set your Santa Muerte in the middle of it.

3. Put the glass of water in front of Santa Muerte, and place the bread and coconut next to it.

4. On the plate, preferably earthenware, place the cross, the coins, and the dollar bill.

5. Next to the plate, put the three apples.

6. Then, light your cigar, take the smoke out of it and apply it to Santa Muerte (three to four times is more than enough). After you have done this, leave the extinguished cigar on top of the apples.

7. Proceed to light two incense cones or sticks and let these burn next to your Santa.

8. Light your candle, preferably with wooden matches, and pray three Our Fathers while making your request with faith and firmness.

9. Your candle must be on as you work. For security reasons, extin-

guish it once you finish working.

10. Fruits, bread, and water should be changed as often as necessary in order to keep the altar fresh and clean.

Similarly, change the flowers and brandy as often as necessary.

For travelers:

What you will need:

1 glass of tequila,
1 statue of Santa Muerte,
1 white tablecloth,
1 red apple,
1 piece of bread or baguette,
1 bottle of Santa Muerte perfume,
1 white plate,
1 shelf (according to personal taste),
1 glass of water,
1 white Santa Muerte candle,
12 coins of your own,
5 white carnations.

Directions:

1. Find an appropriate location for your altar and set up your shelf.

2. Then, put the tablecloth. Remember that this altar should not have any other religious images on it.

3. Proceed to place your Santa Muerte in the middle of your altar.

4. Clean your statue with the perfume of Santa Muerte.

5. Place and light the candle in front of it, and say the following:

"O my Lady, with your divine and infinite power I ask you to free (say your name or the name of the person you want to protect) from all the material and spiritual dangers of so I/she/he may always stay protected and come back safe and sound home. You know well that we admire your power and that is why we ask you never to leave us. So be it."

6. Then, place the ingredients one by one, all except the bread and the coins. These should be on the white plate.

7. Change the ingredients as often as necessary, and never leave the glass of water for more than a week.

..When he came to, the doctors told him that he had a contraction in the spinal discs. They were stuck together and that was what was causing so much pain.

Angel understood exactly what had happened.

He then remembered with a smile the Santa Muerte he had embroidered on the back of his wrestler's mask. And he drifted off into a pleasant sleep.

During that time, Santa Muerte manifested again. Angel felt that he floated and was transported through mountains and lakes. He didn't see anything now either, but he knew that it was she who was speaking to him:

"You must keep fighting, don't be afraid of danger, because I'm going to keep you protected."

Angel smiled confidently.

He clearly heard her voice.

She transmitted serenity and inner peace to him.

And from that moment on, he stopped feeling any pain or discomfort at all, and he knew everything was going to be OK...

Fragment of "In the Arena", story taken from the book
"Testimonies of the Blessed Holy Death",
by Juan Ambrosio and Laila Pita

Rituals

Road Opener: Balm

The use of this balm while invoking Santa Muerte to helps you to open paths, no matter how difficult they may be, as it removes envy, hatred and/or resentment that may exist in your environment, whether that is at work, with friends, with neighbors, or with family.

What you will need:

1 bottle of Unblocking or Road Opener perfume,

1 liter of water or agave liqueur,

1 Santa Muerte candle,

21 bay leaves,

4 liters of water,

9 spearmint branches,

9 rue branches.

Directions:

1. Mix in natural water all the ingredients except the candle. Let it settle for a whole night, covered with a cloth to prevent it from getting dust inside of it.

2. Afterward, move the candle all over your body, starting with the head and ending with the feet, and then say the following prayer:

"Santísima Muerte, I beg you with all my heart that just as God made you immortal and entrusted you to take care of us until we are in the celestial sphere, where we will enjoy of a happy day without night for all eternity, in the name of the Father, the Son, and the Holy Spirit, I beg you and beseech you to deign to be my protector and grant me all the favors that I may ask of you. Amen."

3. Then, proceed to apply a little of this balm all over your body, from head to toe.

It is recommended to do this application before leaving your home, as this will help you to avoid being the target of envy and intrigue.

You should apply this balm as often as you deem necessary.

Love: with flowers

Before performing any ritual with our entity, Santa Muerte, it is necessary to cleanse our environment of negative energies. For that, we will use a mixture of frankincense and myrrh.

What you will need:

1 red candle,

2 white candles,

Ribbon of any color,

Red flowers, carnations or roses,

Bee honey.

Directions:

Pass a white candle through your body, hair, arms, etc., to impregnate it with your body's energy. Then, write your name from top to bottom with a toothpick.

It is very important to have a piece of clothing belonging to the person that we want to influence. Underwear is very effective. If we do not have it, we can use another type of clothes. If you do not have any garments, you can use a photo and put it on the altar.

Pass the candle over the clothing or photograph, and write the person's name with a toothpick from top to bottom.

Once that the two candles are working with their corresponding energies, break a wooden toothpick in half and sharpen both sides.

Join the two white candles by inserting or burying the toothpick in the middle of said candles.

Light the red candle and drip its wax in the cavities of the white candles on both sides so they are more tied together.

Use ribbon to join the two candles by surrounding them with it and making a knot. As you do this, raise your thoughts to Santa Muerte and meditate for a few minutes as you make your request.

When you have finished tying the ribbon, put honey on your fingers and spread it on the two candles.

Then, remove the leaves from the flowers and stick the petals on the candles. Proceed to light the candles.

Lastly, give thanks to Santa Muerte.

Love: the strong kind

What you will need:

1 bay leaf,
2 red-hot charcoals,
2 red candles,
1 censer,
Incense in small bits,
Pink ribbon,
Honey,
Myrrh,
White paper,
Chalk.

Directions:

First of all, set up the altar with: a glass of wine, pieces of chocolate and onion slices in a small plate, and light a 7-Day candle of your choice.

Afterward, light the charcoals and put them in the censer. First, the myrrh in pieces with the frankincense and the bay leaves. This will produce very abundant smoke. Walk all over the place, smoking and purifying the house, as the smoke makes negative charges disappear. It is highly recommended to pass the smoke around the corners of your walls. This procedure HAS two functions:

1) Cleansing your home from negative energies.

2) As the environment is in darkness, the entity of Santa Muerte will enter your house and your statue.

Many people do not know about this and perform rituals without purifying the place first. The place must be clean. Next, pass the smoke through the candles, the ribbon, etc., in order to cleanse them of strange energies.

Next:

Use the chalk and draw a circle around you, including the altar. Leave an opening so you can get out of it and close it. Once you are inside the circle, start performing the ritual. Take one red candles and pass it through your hands, cleansing your hands and charging the candle with your energy. Take the other candle and repeat the process. If you have an element used by the person that you want to influence, pass the candle through that element (it can be a piece of clothing, a photo, etc.), so their energy attaches itself to the candle. If you do not have something from the other person, pass the candle through your hands only, while thinking of them.

Once the candles are charged with energy, proceed to write your full name and date of birth from top to bottom. Next, write with the name of the other person (you can do it with a sharp toothpick).

Smear honey on them to give a touch of sweetness to the work and the relationship (this is ideal for couples that are going through a period of miscommunication or are not together). Once you have smeared the candles with honey, tie the two candles with the ribbon, leaving them joined. Each candle represents one person in the relationship.

Then, light the candles (be careful, candles should always be lit with matches and not with a lighter). Once the candles are lit, write your request on the paper to later burn it in the censer. You can either pray to Santa Muerte or ask her personally as if she was in front of you (when we invoke her, she is with us). Meditate and give thanks to Santa Muerte. Stand up, and with your hands in prayer position, say "Hail Santa Muerte". Open the circle of chalk to let you out, close it again, and let the candles burn out.

Love: to attract the loved one

This ritual should be performed on a Tuesday or Thursday at night, after ten o'clock.

What you will need:

1 bottle of Santa Muerte perfume,
1 jar, preferable earthenware.
1 red quill or a feather,
1 piece of aluminum foil,
1 piece of parchment paper, approximately about 4 inches,
1 Come to Me candle,
1 yard of thin red ribbon,
A small statue of Santa Muerte, preferably red.

Directions:

1. Draw a heart with your marker on the parchment paper (make it large). Write your name and your partner's name diagonally so that these names are crossed.

2. Place your Santísima Muerte in the middle of your heart (it is recommended to use a small statue). Roll up your parchment gradually with the statue inside.

3. Then, tie it with the length of the ribbon. Proceed to pass it over your body several times.

4. Place the roll in the earthenware jar and pour the perfume of Santa Muerte inside of it. Cover the jar with aluminum foil.

5. If you have an altar, this jar should be next to your Santa Muerte statue. Light your union candle and say the following prayer:

"With this candle, I will illuminate my requests and prayers to you, O Lady, O White Sister, so each step that I take day by day gets me nearer the love I'm looking for. And dear Santa Muerte, wherever you are, protect me and deliver me from all evil with your divine power. May this ritual be favorable to me. So be it (the request is made)."

Remember that you must visualize what you are asking for when you are praying.

Once the candle is burnt (which should be next to the jar), place the jar in someplace where no one can see it.

When you see results, place a few red roses and a cigar on Santísima Muerte's altar.

Love: for good luck in love affairs

What you will need:

1 red cloth bag,

1 strainer,

1 bucket,

1 bottle of cinnamon oil,

1 bottle of rose oil,

1 piece of Santeria binding stick,

1 piece of personal clothing (4x4 inches),

1 white plate,

1 small Santa Muerte statue, preferably off-white or white,

1 red candle,

3 red roses (petals only),

Water,

Wooden matches.

Directions:

1. Place in the middle of the altar a piece of your personal clothing (either a shirt, pants, blouse, etc.). Next, place the Santa Muerte on top of the cloth and spread rose petals on top. The Santa Muerte statue must be covered with petals (lay her down).

2. Sprinkle some drops of the oils on the petals and proceed to place the binding stick on top.

3. Cleanse yourself with the red candle from head to toe and light it with the wooden matches. Pray the Santa Muerte prayer (any Santa Muerte prayer that you like can be good).

4. After the candle has been consumed, remove the Santa Muerte from the plate and wrap it, along with your personal clothing, in the red cloth.

5. This wrapping and the binding stick are placed inside the red bag. You should always carry this amulet with you. Very important: you must not let strangers or acquaintances touch it.

6. After that, put the petals on a pot with water to boil. Once the water has boiled, let it rest and cool down so that you can rinse yourself with the water when taking a bath.

Note: Remember that the baths are from the neck down.

Money: to attract it

What you will need:

1 statue of Santa Muerte,

1 white glass plate,

1 white glass candle,

1 green glass candle,

13 gold or silver coins,

White flowers,

Magnet stone with iron filings.

Directions:

Place the statue of the Santísima Muerte on the white plate, putting the 13 coins around the statue. The magnet stone is spread over the coins and sprinkle the iron filings on top of the coins. Write on a piece of Kraft paper the amount of money needed, which will be later burned inside the green glass candle. Light the wick and ask for the amount of money by saying the following prayer:

"Santa Muerte, Helping Spirit, come hear this request. I want money, but not for ambition. I want money for my needs. If you give me this amount within 15 days, I will light this white candle for you ".

When the request is fulfilled, light the white candle to Santa Muerte with a grateful heart.

Money: to attract it with the advice of Santa Muerte

It is advisable to AVOID counting the money or goods you own, as this nullifies the energy of money. Be very careful. Avoid asking for or giving loans. And something very important, never say that you are a jinxed person or state that you do not have money, since what you decree is what appears in your life. Make sure that your words and thoughts are always focused on HAVING money and good resources.

Economic success is in your hands. We only suggest that you manage your energy properly, that way you can generate a steady flow of money. There are other secrets to keeping money:

1. When receiving money that was owed to you, RINSE IT under running tap water. Afterward, dry it with a towel of any color. From now on, this towel will be used solely and exclusively to dry your bills and coins. Do not forget this.

2. Arrange your bills on one side only, so that when you spread them out, not one of them is reversed. Such action will allow you to handle properly the positive energy of prosperity. Try to do the same with coins.

3. When you receive money, cross yourself three times with it. Put it in an envelope intended for the blessing of money. Bless the money and ask for it to multiply.

Money: to have a debt paid off

What you will need:

1 Santa Muerte prayer card,
1 magnet stone,
1 maguey pick,
1 glass sparkling water,
1 Santa Muerte candle, preferably white,
9 cloves of seasoning,
9 guava leaves,
1 bottle of Santa Muerte Perfume.

How to carry out the vigil:

1. Write the name of your debtor on the candle with the maguey pick. Dress it with the Santa Muerte perfume and light it. With all your fervor, pray: "Santísima Muerte, lady of the night, lady of destinies. On this day, I come to you to ask, to beg you to hear my complaint against (name of the person). This person owes me (state the amount). Lady, my mother, for your righteous hand there are no impossibilities, so I ask you with your power to make (name of the person) pay me what he/she owes me.

My Mother, if it were not a difficult situation, I would not dare to ask for your help. But you know my need, my despair. In you, I trust so that what I borrowed will be returned to its rightful hands, so that neither traitors nor liars remain immune, those with seductive tongues who promised to pay and still have to comply. Lady of the night, may your scythe fall relentlessly on the liar. Because you have dominion over life and death, make (name of the person) have no rest, neither in body nor in spirit, until the contracted debt is paid. So be it". (Pray 3 Our Fathers).

2. At the end of your prayer, write the name of the person on the prayer card, as well as the amount owed to you. Do this across the entire length and width of the image and, then, put it under a candle.

3. Finally, put the guava leaves, the magnet stone, and the cloves inside the glass of sparkling water. Place the preparation next to the candle. Let the candle burn completely. Throw the remaining paraffin in the trash can and pour the sparkling water at the entrance of your debtor's house (or on top of this photograph).

4. Do this ritual as many times as necessary until you get your money back.

Money: for your partner to help with debts

This ritual is very effective for your partner to help you with the maintenance of the house and children. You can also use it if you are divorced and need alimony.

What you will need:

1 dollar bill from your partner (borrow it from him/her),

1 eggshell (clean and pulverized),

1 tablespoon of ground mustard,

1 statue of Santa Muerte, preferably in amber color,

1 green Santa Muerte candle.

Directions:

Cleanse your entire body from head to toe with the candle. Light it on a plate, preferably earthenware, and say the prayer:

"Jesus Christ victor who was conquered on the cross, conquer (name of the person), who shall be defeated with me. In the name of the Lord, I beg you (say the name) to become aware of the needs of this household and to open their pockets and their heart to support us with generosity.

Santísima Muerte, I beg you earnestly, that just as you are an immortal god, until we find ourselves in the celestial sphere, where we shall enjoy a happy day without night for all eternity, and in the name of the Father, the Son, and the Holy Spirit: I beg you and I beseech you to deign to be my protector and grant me all the favors that I ask from you until the last day, hour, and moment when His Divine Majesty orders you to take me to His presence. Amen".

Make your request with faith.

Spread a little eggshell powder along with the ground mustard on the dollar bill, fold it in three parts and put it under the earthenware plate. Leave it there until the candle is consumed.

Afterward, place the bill in your purse to establish a link with your partner's money.

The ritual can be done any day of the week with the sole exception of Sunday morning.

Money: Ritual # 1

What you will need:

1 dollar bill (it must be yours, not borrowed),
1 red cloth bag,
1 white quartz,
1 silver Santa Muerte pendant,
1 plate, preferably earthenware.
1 bag of iron filing,
1 white Santa Muerte candle,
9 coins (yours).

Directions:

1. Place all the ingredients on your earthenware plate.

2. Light your candle, say the prayer of your choice to Santa Muerte, and make your request, whatever you wish.

3. Place the plate next to the candle and leave it for two days.

4. On the third day, place all the ingredients inside the red bag.

5. You should always carry this bag with you, in the right side pocket of your pants, on your bag, or your purse.

6. The candle should be left until it is completely consumed.

Money: Ritual # 2

What you will need:

1 statue of Santa Muerte, preferably golden,
1 set of dice,
1 piece of Kraft paper,
1 piece of sky-blue cloth,
7 gold-colored coins.

Directions:

1. Roll two dice in front of your statue of Santa Muerte and write down the sum of numbers on a piece of parchment paper. Also write down your first and last name and the sum of your date of birth (e.g. December 2, 1975 equals $1 + 2 + 2 + 1 + 9 + 7 + 5 = 27$). Fold the paper and place it under the image in front of a mirror and cover with a piece of light blue cloth.

2. Place seven golden coins in the shape of a cross between the image and the mirror and repeat this spell: "Santa Muerte increases my money, increases my gold, increases my coins, increases my treasure, increases my wealth and prosperity."

3. Lastly, bury the coins and the paper wrapped in the cloth at the foot of a tree with many leaves and repeat the previous chant.

Money: smoke recipe to bring in money

This is a very effective ritual for all those who want to increase their economic power in a short period of time. It is a very easy recipe, but it must be done with a lot of faith to obtain optimal results.

Cases in which it is used:

1) I want to get extra money because I am in financial difficulties.

2) I need a bonus to meet a series of upcoming expenses.

3) I am waiting to receive a long-overdue payment and I want to receive it now!

What you will need:

1 tablespoon of cinnamon,

1 small pot with a handle,

2 tablespoons of sugar,

8 or 10 coffee beans.

To make this recipe, you must remember that it is not necessary to find a specific day and time. It is best to make it on a Tuesday, but you can also make it whenever it is necessary.

Directions:

1. Place the small pot on the stove, with the coffee, sugar and cinnamon inside of it. Once a lot of smoke starts to come out, pick it up carefully and carry the pot around each room of the house.

2. First, you have to say your name and surname, and then repeat the following prayer:

"Santísima Muerte, powerful protector both in life and after it, grant me your protection in every act of my life just as God granted you immense virtues. That I may obtain everything that I want, need or is convenient for me. May it suffice for me to implore your sacred name or devotion. Mighty Lady of Death. As this is a means of protection for my house and my family (name the people who live in the house), this spell will accomplish my goals. Amen."

Then, ask for whatever you need to cover household expenses or whatever is needed, and repeat the following:

"May the money enter my home with ease to cover all my needs in abundance, with the help of God and Santa Muerte. Amen."

Finish the tour of the house at the door of the home. Go outside and make the sign of the cross three times with the little pot when no one is around. You have to think that the money will enter your home from today onwards.

Notes:

—Clean the container, remove the remains, and reuse it only for this ritual.

—You can do the ritual twice a month and even more if it is very urgent.

Cleansings: for the home, business, office, or workshop

This should be done every week in the premises, office or workshop where you want to do the cleansing.

What you will need:

1 statue of Santa Muerte,

7 rosemary sprigs,

7 white candles,

Water from seven churches or holy water bought from the store,

A little vodka.

Directions:

1. Place the statue of Santa Muerte on an altar and light a white candle.

2. Empty the water from the seven churches into a container, then place the 7 rosemary sprigs in it, as well as the vodka and let the mixture untouched for 7 days.

3. Leave the container with the mixture in front of the statue of Santa Muerte.

At the end of the indicated time, pour the water in your business and repeat the following prayer 7 times:

"Blessed rosemary of consecrated God that was born and not sown. Blessed rosemary, by the virtue that God has given you, I ask that the good may enter and all the bad may leave."

Finally, pray an Our Father and three Hail Marys, and Santa Muerte will always be by your side to help you.

Protection with the Hand of Santa Muerte

What you will need:

1 new needle,

1 statue of Santa Muerte, with articulated hands,

1 sheet of white paper,

1 white Santa Muerte candle,

Tobacco of any kind.

How to perform the ritual:

On a Friday at noon, write your greatest wish on the white candle with the new needle. This wish can be for work, money, personal success, difficult love, family, or private obstacles and/or protection, or for general good luck.

Then, write it with black or blue ink on the paper and place the tobacco on it. Make a small cylindrical packet (as if it were a cigar) that you can glue with a little paraffin or beeswax or Campeche wax. You should not use adhesive tape or any other plastic glue.

Put the roll of paper with your wish in Santa Muerte's right hand, which is the articulated hand that can be moved.

Light the candle and place it in front of Santa Muerte. Say the prayer of your choice, and ask with all your heart for your wish to be fulfilled.

Protection: with the Five-Pointed Star

What you will need:

13 white or red candles,

1 handful of coarse grain salt,

1 small mirror,

1 piece of white paper,

Cane alcohol.

How to perform the ritual:

1. At three in the morning, light thirteen white or red candles, depending on the desired effect.

2. Place the thirteen candles in a circle on the ground and light them.

3. While the candles are burning, form a five-pointed star with coarse grain salt. Place a mirror in the center of the star and the remaining salt on top of the mirror.

4. Before the candles start to extinguish on their own, recite the prayer of the Santa Muerte.

5. The petition must be written on a blank piece of paper, as well as the name of the person you are working with.

6. When only one candle remains lit, put a good amount of cane alcohol on the salt, light it with fire from the last candle, and burn the written paper as you wait for the mirror to break. This indicates that what has been asked for will be done without delay.

Note #1: This ritual should be done in a patio or a place where it is safe to light the candles and burn the salt.

Note #2: This ritual should not be done more than three times in a row, as it is strong enough to cause a disturbance for the practitioner because of the accumulated energy.

Protection: with the Three Deaths

What you will need:

1 censer, preferably earthenware.

1 special Santa Muerte tablecloth,
Tortilla ash,

1 plate, preferably earthenware.

1 Santa Muerte candle,

3 statues of Santa Muerte: black, white, and red,

Incense composed of myrrh, copal, and storax.

How to perform the ritual:

This ritual shall be done on the 9th of each month. It is recommended to do it in September, since it is the ninth month.

Start at nine o'clock at night. You should not eat meat or drink alcoholic beverages during the day in which you will perform the ritual. If possible, take a bath before starting.

1. Place the white Santa Muerte tablecloth. You can either buy it or make it (it has or should have an image of Santa Muerte in the middle with black thread or yarn. If you do not have it, you can just place the statue of Santa Muerte in the middle of the tablecloth). Place the earthenware censer on the embroidery or print and burn some incense while asking at the same time for Santa Muerte to accept you as her protégé.

2. Then, place the three images of Santa Muerte around the censer, forming a triangle. At the head, you will put the white or bone-colored Santa Muerte. On the left, put the black statue. On the right, put the red one.

3. The censer should be in the center.

4. Say the following prayer:

The Protective Scythe:

"My White Girl, I prostrate myself at your feet to ask you, to beg you, to make your strength, your power and your omnipotence be felt against those who will attempt to destroy me.

My White Girl, I implore you to be my shield and my protection against evil. May your protective scythe cut the obstacles that stand in the way.

My Child, may the closed doors open and the open roads may be shown.

My adored one, there is no evil that you cannot overcome, no impossible thing that will not bend to your will. I surrender myself to you."

5. At the beginning of the prayer, light the candle placed behind the white statue of Santa Muerte. This candle should be placed on an earthenware plate.

6. After nine minutes of lighting the candle, pick up the image and write your name with the index finger of your hand on the tablecloth by using ash from the burned tortilla.

7. Place the image so that it covers the part of the tablecloth that you wrote on.

8. Say the prayer again and wait nine minutes. Pick up the red image and write your name in another corner, with the tortilla ash. Wait the same time and repeat the process with the black image.

9. At the end, each image should cover the part of the tablecloth where your name was written in. With the remaining ash, write your name again under one of the folds of the tablecloth so that it is not visible. Above and below your name, write Santa Muerte's name so that it looks like this:

"Santa Muerte",

Your name,

"Santa Muerte."

10. At the end, leave a special offering to Santa Muerte. It can be a flower, something to eat, fruit, mezcal, or tequila. It should be an offering that you must always leave, so choose something that you always have on hand in your home.

Protection: against disagreements

To settle disagreements within the family, you will need:

1 container,
1 piece of white paper and pencil,
1 blue candle,
1 white candle,
Wooden matches,
Incense,
Aluminum foil

Directions:

1. On the blank paper, write the names and surnames of the members of the family nucleus. Put the ones with the worst temper at the beginning.

2. Once everything is written, place the paper in the container. Light the candles with the matches (not with another candle): the blue one first and the white one at last. Stick them on top of a plate with a little wax.

3. Once this is done, light the incense and place it in said container. Go around each room carrying an image of Santa Muerte, the candles and the incense. Stay in each room for a few seconds, and say the following prayer:

"Santísima Muerte, you who illuminate my path so I may reach an ideal outcome, you who give me the divine gift of forgiving and forgetting all the evil that is done to me, and you who are with me at every moment of my life, I want, in this short prayer, to thank you for everything and to confirm once again that I will never separate myself from you. Protect us. May there be peace with my loved ones now and in eternal glory. Amen."

4. The ritual should be done for three days. On the first and second times, the candles are left to burn for approximately one hour, and on the third time, they are left to burn in their entirety.

5. Once the candles have been consumed, collect what is left in the container and wrap it in aluminum foil. Burry it on the ground.

Note # 1: No extra request should be made. Just do the ritual, think strongly about harmony and family well-being.

Note # 2: The best time to do the ritual would be midnight, although it is not essential.

Protection: against negative energy # 1

If you are an easy target for envy, harassment, or bad vibes, both at home and at work, we suggest that you follow this ritual.

An appropriate day to do so is the first Friday of the month.

What you will need:

1 mirror (square, as this represents the four elements with which the Santísima Muerte works),

1 prayer card of Santa Muerte,

1 bottle of Road Opener perfume,

1 bottle of Santa Muerte perfume,

1 plate, preferably earthenware,

1 piece of charcoal,

White glue.

Directions:

Glue the picture of Santa Muerte on the mirror with a little glue. Then, light the charcoal and place it on the earthenware plate. Pour a few drops of the Santa Muerte and Road Opener perfume on the coal. You will start seeing aromatic smoke coming out of it. Pass the mirror through the smoke and say this prayer:

"O Santísima Muerte I call you, I implore you, so that with your power you withdraw (say the name of the person who causes you problems), that envy and bad luck may be removed from me and that with this mirror see reflected and removed all witchcraft, Santeria work, voodoo, palo Mayombe, black magic, or any jinx that could cause me any harm. Thank you, my Lady ".

You can make any personal request. Remember that you must put all your faith and spiritual firmness into this ritual.

The consecrated mirror is placed at the entrance of your home or business so that it faces and reflects any person who enters (this will serve to repel any bad energy). The burning charcoal is left to burn until it goes out by itself, which will serve to purify your home or business.

Protection: against negative energy # 2

What you will need:

1 mirror,

1 Santa Muerte medal,

4 white candles,

9 sticks of sandalwood incense.

Directions:

1. Stick the medal in the center of the mirror. You can do it with adhesive cloth or Campeche wax.

2. Place the candles on all four sides of the mirror and light them.

3. Say the following prayer:

"Blessed Santa Muerte, fortress against my enemies: today, I ask you to keep all envy, gossip, or evil away from me. May all negative desires of those around me be returned to their owner. Santa, may your eyes be my eyes and may your punishment be mine against whoever for evil or for money wants to harm me or speak ill of me. On you, I leave the retribution of their actions. Blessed Santa Muerte, fortress against my enemies, in your hands I commend myself".

4. Ask that all evil may be rejected through the mirror and that all envy may be dissolved and transmuted.

5. When the candles are consumed, place the mirror at the main entrance of your home or business, inside.

6. Light the incense sticks and put them in every room, including bathroom and kitchen.

Note: This ritual can be done several times with the same mirror. You will only have to replace the candles and incense.

Protection: against caused diseases

What you will need:

1 purple cloth bag,
1 tablespoon of camphor powder,
1 tablespoon of musk,
1 tablespoon of 9 different kinds of seeds,
1 Santa Muerte pendant,
1 meter of purple ribbon,
1 piece of virgin parchment paper,
1 jet stone,
1 maguey pick,
1 Healing candle.

Directions:

1. Mix all the seeds, camphor, and musk and put them in the purple bag.

2. Then, write the names of all the members of your family on the paper, starting with the eldest to the youngest.

3. Place your jet stone in the middle of the paper and tie it with the purple ribbon. Once tied, ask and visualize your family filled with peace, health, and love. Place inside your bag this scroll along with the Santa Muerte pendant.

4. Write the names of all the members of your family all over your candle with the maguey pick.

5. Light the candle and pray the printed prayer on it, asking for health and wealth.

6. It is recommended that, when your candle is on, you place your purple bag next to it. That way, it will be filled with energy through the candle.

7. Once it is consumed, place the bag at the entrance of your house, as it will serve as a safeguard and protection.

Protection: during a pending trial

It must be done at the altar of Santa Muerte. If this is not possible, you should always visualize Santa Muerte while performing this ritual.

What you will need:

1 small bottle of Santa Muerte perfume,

1 piece of Road Opener Santeria stick,

1 piece of 6-inch white paper,

1 black ink pen,

1 packet of Santa Muerte powder,

1 yard of white hemp thread,

9 Santa Muerte candles or 9 white candles.

Directions:

1. Apply the Santa Muerte perfume to all the candles and proceed to sprinkle each and every candle with the powder. Write on the paper the number of the trial or case and the name of your opponent with the black pen.

2. Proceed to roll up the paper together with the stick and tie it very well with the help of the hemp thread.

3. Leave it tied next to Santa Muerte. Light one candle per day, praying the Santa Muerte prayer.

4. Every person who lights a candle must make their requests, asking for their paths to be opened in the problem or legal judgment that is pending, requesting that you come out well and free from all legal problems.

5. Once the 9 days are over, bury the tied stick in a flowerpot and offer Santa Muerte some white roses, requesting and thanking in advance for your wishes to be fulfilled.

Health: to cast out all diseases # 1

What you will need:

9 blue candles.

1 photograph of the person for whose health you are praying for.

Directions:

1. Starting on a Tuesday, for 9 days in a row, you will light a blue candle in front of the altar of Santa Muerte.

2. Next to it, you will place the photograph of the person for whose health you are praying for. After doing the Santa Muerte prayer, you should visualize the person being healthy and without any type of disease.

3. You can also pass the candle all over the sick person's body.

Note: If you want to take care of your personal health, just put the blue candle permanently on the altar along with the normal white Santa Muerte candle.

Health: to eradicate all diseases # 2

If you are going to perform this ritual, it is suggested that you do it in front of a statue of Santa Muerte. If you do not have one, you can do it in front of a prayer card.

With this ritual, you will cleanse yourself of all diseases, whether natural or caused.

What you will need:

1 bottle of Santa Muerte perfume,

1 statue of Santa Muerte,

1 Santa Muerte soap,

1 magnet stone,

1 white rose (petals only),

1 Miraculous Healer or Healer candle,

1 gallon of tap water.

Directions:

1. Mix the perfume, the petals, and the stone in the gallon of water. This water should be left next to your Santa Muerte statue for 24 hours.

2. Bathe as usual using the soap, and proceed to use the mixture to rinse (if the water is too cold, you can add hot water to warm it up). Each time that you rinse, visualize yourself vibrating with health and prosperity. Your body will be spiritually cleansed.

3. Dress in white. This ritual is best done first thing on a Monday morning.

4. Regarding the candle, you should cleanse your body from top to bottom (passing the candle over the most affected area).

5. Light your candle and pray an Our Father and the prayer printed on your candle. At the end, make your request with faith and firmness.

6. Place your candle in front of your Santa Muerte statue or on your altar. Light it and let it consume.

HEALTH: to heal from all evil

What you will need:

1 bottle of Santa Muerte perfume,

1 yard of purple ribbon,

1 black ink pen,

1 maguey pick,

1 cigar,

1 medium bunch of rue,

1 Health candle.

Directions:

1. Write all your discomforts along the ribbon with a black ink pen. Tie the rue with this ribbon, forming a bouquet.

2. Apply a little of the Santa Muerte perfume to the whole rue bouquet.

3. Light the cigar and apply its smoke to the rue bouquet.

4. Proceed to cleanse your entire body with the rue, from head to toe, repeatedly passing the bouquet over the most affected area.

5. Then, wrap the bouquet in a newspaper and throw it in the trash can, visualizing that you are throwing away the disease and as if all the symptoms that you wrote down were being thrown out once and for all.

6. Write your full name across the width of your candle with the maguey pick. Cleanse your entire body with the candle, from head to toe (passing over the most affected area).

7. Light your candle and say the prayer printed on the candle. It should be lit in front of your Santa Muerte or placed on your altar, but always pray to her for your health.

Repeat this ritual as often as necessary.

Health: for a loved one

When we have a family member or close friend in a clinic or hospital, we can help them with the following ritual.

In front of our statue of the Santísima Muerte, will light a candle of the Santísima Muerte. It is recommended to be a purple or blue statue.

Put the name of the sick person on three sides of the candle. The name shall be written three times, distributed so that each name is more or less at the same distance from the other. (It does not have to be exact).

On the back of the candle, place the name of the hospital where he/she is being hospitalized or the place where he/she is living. In front of the candle, place a prayer card of the Santa Muerte. Pray the following prayer for 7 days:

"Santísima Muerte, protector, owner, and mistress of life, angel that our Father created to help and serve.

Today, I implore you, I beg you to grant health and life to (say the sick person's name). May his/her days on earth endure. May his/her body regain vigor and energy. You who can do all things, save him/her and bring him/her back to health.

I implore you. I ask you this day and this hour, through Jesus Christ victorious on the Cross, that (name) be healed, and bring him/her back. Amen."

Once the seven days are over, thank the Santa Muerte. Pick up the prayer card and give it to the person for whom this ritual was performed.

It is recommended that a candle is always lit until the patient is recovered.

Rodrigo's wife, sensing that something bad was happening, entrusted herself to her Santa Muerte, and praying non stop, she begged her to return him safe and sound.

Several men organized a search party for her husband. The anguished lady gave one of her friends a picture of the Holy Death.

"Here, take her with you for protection."

The friend received the picture just so as not to offend the lady. He did not believe in such things, but this was not the time to go into clarification.

It was already about one or two in the morning when everything happened, at the moment that Rodrigo was spinning on a free fall, he clearly saw that image that his wife loved so much, the skeleton dressed in a washed red tunic, surrounded by skulls and he felt safe.

Later, after he was rescued, he would remember that the image glowed as if it had its own light...

Fragment of the story: "Miracle on the Mountain", taken from the book "Testimonies of the Blessed Holy Death", by Juan Ambrosio and Laila Pita

Prayers

The Niña Bonita (The Pretty Girl) and her Commandments

There are 10 commandments about how to serve and respect the cult of Santa Muerte, namely:

Pay attention:

1. You shall worship Santa Muerte with all respect.
2. You shall not swear in vain using her name.
3. You shall adore her on her feast days.
4. You shall honor all your religious brothers.
5. You shall not harm anyone, not even yourself.
6. You shall not commit acts that harm our worship of Santa Muerte.
7. You shall not abuse your spiritual knowledge.
8. You shall not give false testimonies related to her.
9. You shall not use her name to scam others.
10. You shall not desire other people's wealth.

Praise

O Santa Muerte! You who are God's messenger, who are so close to Him, keep with you the stealth of the nights, the hope of the dawns, and the acceptance of the sunsets.

You are the one who waits patiently in the dark for God to give you the final command. You are the one who lovingly embraces the souls that you must lead back to the light.

You are the one who harvests spirits and guides them to their final destination when the Creator has so determined.

But you are also the one who respectfully turns away when He decides to give a second chance to those whose prayers are heard and answered.

It is you who protects those whose turn has yet to come.

It is you who accompanies those of us who believe in you and advises us and counsel us during our journey in this world.

It is you, Santa Muerte, who gives herself faithfully to all who venerate and invoke you.

It is you whom I love and respect. Blessed be, relentless Mistress of Darkness.

Altar: before starting a ritual

O Santísima Muerte, I invoke you so that through your image you may free me from all dangers, whether material or spiritual, and through this sacred flame my body is cleansed of all negativity or curse. May love, peace, and wealth flow into my life. So be it".

Love: to attract the loved one

"Santa Muerte, helper of the brothers who are without love. I invoke you to attract (say the name of the desired person) to my life, so that through love and happiness he/she may be the one who fills my soul with peace and tranquility. The virtues of the entire universe are deposited in the divine energy that flows within my heart, as God the Heavenly Father will help to make this happen."

Once the prayer is finished, you should light a red candle to attract that loved one with love. Pray three Our Fathers and this prayer every day:

"Dear Muerte of my heart, do not forsake me of your protection and I ask for your blessing to this devotee of yours so that, in return, success and prosperity may come to my person and my economy. Take away all diseases, natural or provoked. So be it."

Good fortune: in business and home

(If you say this prayer, Santa Muerte will help you in your sales and the peace of your home).

"Dear Muerte of my heart, do not forsake me of your protection and, from this moment, cover my home, work, or business. May you attract white energies from the universe so that nothing is ever lacking and that all our needs are covered by the divine energy of God the Father, God the Son, and God the Holy Spirit. Amen.

By the virtues that you possess, I will be able to overcome all the obstacles and I will not be interposed by people who bring evil, but by positive people who only know how to love and respect all human beings that inhabit this planet. I do not aspire for riches, but a fair life without a lack of anything. Protect me night and day ".

(Afterward, pray three Our Fathers and light a white candle to express gratitude for the favors of God the Father).

Good Luck: Spell

You can light a cigar (preferably, but if it is difficult to get, you can get a cigarette instead).

Light the cigar or cigarette and put it in an ashtray to burn in front of an image of Santa Muerte, either a statue or a prayer card.

"In the name of the great Power of God the Father, Son, and Holy Spirit. I (say your name) offer the smoke of this tobacco for the Eternal Father to give me the strength and power to overcome obstacles and enemies.

For our Santa Muerte to put a mantle of light on my path.

For the brothers of the white mansion to make me white and pure.

For the brothers of light to always accompany me.

For the wise Solomon to give me wisdom.

For the Lord Christ to cleanse my body of any bad fluids and clean my house (business, love relationship ...) of bad influences.

For Santa Clara to clarify the roads and let me see with clarity what I need to know in all my deals (business or otherwise),

For my protective spirit to always be with me, protecting me.

For Don Juan of the Red Cape, Don Juan of the Blue Cape, Don Juan of the Yellow Cape, Don Juan of the White Cape, so they may protect me with their capes and accompany me wherever I go.

I offer the smoke of this tobacco for Don Juan of Triumph to help me to succeed in everything that I undertake. For Don Juan of Success and Prosperity to give me success and prosperity.

For Don Juan of Love, that I may always be surrounded by love.

I offer the smoke of this tobacco for Don Juan of Money to give me a lot of money, silver to spend, copper to distribute, and gold for my treasure.

I offer the smoke of this tobacco to Santa Muerte, San Expedito, San Benito, to the Swords of San Miguel, and Santa Bárbara. May they cut the obstacles that might appear in my way. So be it. Amen."

Pray three Our Fathers.

Good luck: to attract it

"By the virtue that God gave you, my dear Santa Muerte, I want you to free me from all evil spells, dangers, and diseases, and to give me LUCK, HAPPINESS, and MONEY in return.

I want you to give me friends and free me from enemies."

Note: If you need to reconcile with someone, add this last verse:

"And make (say the name) come humbly before me to ask for my forgiveness, meek as a lamb faithful to its promises, always loving and submissive for life. Amen."

Pray three Our Fathers.

Family conflicts: ending them

"When it is night and we are not looking, your silver gleam irradiates the heavy black clouds. Throw away the germ of evil with your breath, Santa Muerte. Remove the chains of matter from the thoughts of the people of my house, O Holy Death, help me to see clarity in the darkness. Cut the ears of evil with your scythe. Let joy return to my home with Justice. Dilute whatever damage may have been caused. Cleanse us of all evil. Amen."

Money: abundance and finances

"Heavenly and Gracious Muerte, I pray for you to bless me and my family with abundance and well-being. I know that you recognize that a family is more than the father, mother, sister or brother, wife, husband, sons or daughters, but everyone who also believes and trusts in you.

Santa Muerte, I make this prayer to ask for your blessing in finances, not only for me but for everyone who is praying.

And may the power of the group prayer made by everyone who believes and trusts you reach us all. I thank you for the blessings already received and for those that are yet to come.

Santa Muerte, free the people who are now fighting for their families from their debts and economic pressures.

Give me your divine wisdom to be a good instrument of all that you have entrusted to me.

Santa Muerte, for I know how wonderful you are and how you bless us if we obey your word and live by it. If we have faith, like the size of a mustard seed, we will see how you send us your blessings.

I thank you, Lady, for the recent blessings that I have received and for the future blessings, for I know that you will bless us even more. In your name, I pray. Amen."

Money: to get rid of debts

Candles: A green candle to attract prosperity and a purple candle to promote good profits.

Other elements: Place coins or bills in use between the candles, next to an image of Santa Muerte.

Time of day to perform the ritual: In the evening. Prayer:

"O Santísima Muerte, let money come into this house. May I be able to pay all my commitments on time, may I be able to give my family the well-being that they need and deserve. After paying everything on time, may there be money left in my wallet to help whoever you put in my way and whoever needs it.

In return, I promise to do good and to help those who need it without greed or envy dwelling in my soul. Amen."

(Repeat 3 times.)

Money: to arrive promptly

Buy a glass candle with the image of Santa Muerte stamped on it or a candle with the figure of Santa Muerte.

On the top, put honey, a little cinnamon powder, and three coins. Proceed to light the candle and pray the prayer to Santa Muerte and three Our Fathers while asking for the arrival of the money you need.

Money: prosperity in business

"Great Lady of Light:

I invoke you to enlighten my business and my economy.

You are and will be my protector. Give me the strength to move forward.

And may my fortune multiply day by day. May my work meet all my material needs.

Thank you, my Lady, for listening to me and especially for (make the request). Amen ".

Money: when someone owes you money

Buy a black candle. On one of its sides, write the name of the person who owes you the money. On the other side of the candle, write the same name again in reverse. For example, if the person is called Mario López, you should write "zepol oiram".

Once this is done, every night you have to pray the classic prayer "Jesus Christ victor who was conquered on the cross" and say the name of the person who owes you money. After the prayer, ask in your own words to the Santísima Muerte that the money that belongs to you comes back and that she protects you from all evil.

Money: overcoming difficulties

"Santa Muerte, you who own the whole universe and have endowed the Earth with enough riches to feed all the men who inhabit it, come to our aid.

Lady, you care for the lilies of the field and the birds of the sky, you clothe them, nourish them and make them prosper, manifest your motherly providence over us.

Help us, Lady, since our salvation can only come from honest and good men, may you instill in the hearts of our neighbors a sense of justice, honesty, and charity.

Take care of our family, who is confidently awaiting its daily bread.

Strengthen our bodies.

Take away our worries and our anxieties. Give serenity to our life, so that we may correspond more easily to your divine grace and feel your motherly love watching over us. Amen."

Invocation to Santa Muerte

"Lady of Death, ethereal spirit, most powerful and implacable.

Indispensable in the moment of danger, I invoke you, confident of your goodness. Pray for Almighty God to grant me everything that I ask of you.

May those who would do me harm or give me the evil eye regret for their whole life and that everything that these people sow on the spiritual plane, may return to them multiplied.

For those who owe me something, I ask you to bring it back to me and if they ignore your command, good spirit of Death, make them feel uneasy until they return and fulfill their promise or pending debt.

I name you my lawyer in employment and business, and please prosper with me everyone who honors our dealings. But if they were to make deals that would harm me behind my back, I pray for you to make everything go backward for them and to lose and lose until they understand the evil of their ways and correct them.

O Lady of Death, my guardian angel, I trust you. Amen!"

To ask for advice

This prayer has to be said at night before going to sleep when you are worried about a problem.

Before you begin to pray, think carefully about the issue for which you are requesting advice. If possible, ask one or more questions to be answered. For example, if you want to move your business to a certain location, you can say:

"Santa Muerte, I want to move my business to such-and-such street and such-and-such number. Give me your advice. Tell me if the place is convenient for me. Will I have good customers in that place? Will my business be safe at that address? Will the owner of the place be a good landlord? "

And after you finish asking your questions, start praying:

"In your dark empire, Santa Muerte, I implore your presence to ask for your advice.

Give me your advice. Speak through my left ear. Tell me what to do if the horizon is uncertain and the future fearful.

Give me your advice.

A dream may be the way for me to receive your message. A stranger starting a conversation with me may be your envoy. A document sent to me or found by me may be the clue that you are marking for me. In short, I will be open to receiving an answer by whatever means or channel you want to use.

Give me your message. I am waiting for you."

Family problems: finding the solution

"Those who have entered your lordship know that you always wait for them, that you are patient, and that you know your mission!

Those of us who are awaiting, we look beyond, we fear, we suffer, and we laugh.

Santa Muerte, show a glimpse of your wisdom to allow me to find the idea that will end this problem.

I know that the solution to my problem is in front of me, but my eyes do not see it. Remove the blindfold, come.

I bring you these white flowers in gratitude for your generous protection."

(At the end of the prayer, place 9 white flowers in front of the statue of Santa Muerte and light a white candle).

Protection of children

"Do not forget, Holy Lady of Death, that you were also an infant.

In the depths of the temporal abysses, there is a record of your legends as an infant.

The childhood of your holy concept was already inferred from power, your grace already had mercy. I ask you lovingly, Santa Muerte, to take care of (say the children's name).

Let only good things happen to them. Lay down your mantle to protect them from all sources of danger. Take care of their health and help them to be good people. Make their heart clear and balanced. May their thoughts be prudent and determined. Give them the sensitivity to appreciate and respect the wonder of the Creator's great work, including all His creatures, animal, human, or divine. Amen".

Protection to the business

"I have this thanks to you, Lady of the dark abysses. Avert all evil presence, repel the traitor and bring closer those who come accompanied by love and goodwill.

Expel from here, all envy and all the wicked who could come with it. Point with your holy finger where I should go. Protect me from all risks. Attract fortune amassed with the work of my being. Let enough wealth to enter through this door so that I may continue the mission that you have entrusted to me. Amen."

Protection against theft

"Santa Muerte, I ask for your protection. Keep thieves away from these doors. Cover the four walls of my space with your white mantle. Cast out the intruders who could come here with bad intentions. Protect our belongings. Guard these ceilings and walls against bad wills. Do not allow lost spirits to lead their followers here. Guard my home and my business, and surround them with good people and things. I cast these coins in your honor. Amen".

(Throw 9 coins into the air and leave them there).

Protection of your job

"Holy Lady of Death, my presence in this world is brief but protected by you.

I beg you, O Lady of Darkness, to let this humble follower keep working to sustain myself and my family.

Come to my aid. Disrupt every circumstance that could affect me. Drive envy away and grant me health. Amen."

(Pray every night and light a Santa Muerte candle on the 9th day until the request is achieved.)

Protection during travel

Santísima Muerte, I invoke your holy name to ask you to help me in this endeavor. Facilitate my passing on mountains, valleys, and roads. Walk beside me at dawn, at dusk, and also at nightfall.

Stay with me at all times during my journey, so that evil instincts vanish before me by your mighty Protection. Santa Muerte, make the problems diminish until they disappear. Make my body healthy before, during, and also after the trip.

Open your wings so that during my journey, myself and those who go with me or cross my path may be safe. Let all paths open brightly before me under your protection. Give me wisdom and patience to reach my destination on time.

I also ask you to advise the elements to be kind to me during my journey, for I want to travel in a happy environment, under an open sky, with a kind and gentle sun and a soft breeze to cool down my forehead and remind me of the wonder of nature. Amen"

(Light a yellow candle a few days before you leave on your trip. When you return, light a red candle to give thanks for having arrived back safely).

To get rid of a vice

"Santísima Muerte of Moonlight.

You who dominate the earthly plane.

You who promote bliss and who remind us that the purpose of this life is happiness before you arrive to collect us.

Santísima Muerte of Moonlight, I beg you to remove all vice or excess from my life and the lives of my loved ones. Bring peace of mind to my home.

Allow (say your name or the name of the person that you want to help) to stop abusing (state the form of vice, addiction, or abuse).

To regain sobriety and temperance.

Help (repeat the name of the person) to drop the blindfold from their eyes so that transformation finds its true path.

Show clearly the reasons why vice should not nest in their hearts, so that it does not devour their inner light. Place your moon-colored wings on their spirit so they feel your powerful presence.

Santísima Muerte of Moonlight, I beg you to remove all vice or excess from my life and the lives of my loved ones. Bring peace of mind to my home.

I spread seven seeds in the earth and let your name fertilize the decision that will lead to new situations that will open the doors of light through respect and love.

Santísima Muerte of Moonlight, I beg you to remove all vice or excess from my life and the lives of my loved ones. Bring peace of mind to my home. I leave everything in your hands. Amen."

Health for the body

"Santísima Muerte, protector, owner, and mistress of life, angel that our Father created to help and serve.

Today, I implore you, I beg you to grant health and life to (say the sick person's name). May his/her days on earth endure. May his/her body regain vigor and energy. You who can do all things, save him/her and bring him/her back to health.

I implore you. I ask you this day and this hour, through Jesus Christ victorious on the Cross, be moved and bring him/her back. Amen."

Seven-day prayer

These are seven powerful prayers to be prayed for seven days.

"In the name of the Father,

of the Son, and of the Holy Spirit.

Immaculate Santa Muerte, being of light,

I beg you to grant me favors

that I may ask you until the last day, hour, and moment

when His Divine Majesty

orders you to bring me before

His presence.

Muerte, dearest to my heart,

do not forsake me with your protection."

MONDAY

"Santa Muerte, at the beginning of this week I ask for you to fill my family, my home, and my work with blessings. Protect me from all evil. So be it."

TUESDAY

"White Girl, I prostrate myself at your feet and I ask you earnestly to

79

grant me health. Keep away any disease so that I may move forward. I ask this with all my heart."

WEDNESDAY

"Today, I will not ask you for anything. But I do want to thank you for the protection that you offer to me and my loved ones. Continue to cover us under your mantle. Thank you, thank you, thank you."

THURSDAY

"Today, before I leave, I ask you to open all the paths that will lead me to live peacefully. I do not ask for great luxuries, only that you give me what is necessary to live without worries. I place my faith in you."

FRIDAY

"White Sister, I ask for you to give me wisdom through the owl that always accompanies you, so I may know how to guide my children (family) and may they always know how to behave as good beings. In you, I trust."

SATURDAY

"Thank you, my Santita, for allowing me to see the light of a new day. In gratitude, I promise to think of you. And I offer you an Our Father and a Hail Mary and Glory Be, so that my requests may be heard. Thank you for all that you give me. In you, I trust. Amen."

SUNDAY

"Thank you, Santísima Muerte, for being close to me the seven days of this week. Thank you for giving me protection and keeping away from me and my home any evil that may haunt us. My devotion is forever yours. Amen."

Rosary to Santa Muerte

HOW TO PRAY IT

1. Make the sign of the cross and pray the Apostles' Creed or the Act of Contrition.
2. Pray an Our Father.
3. Pray three Hail Marys and Glory Be.
4. Announce the first mystery. Pray an Our Father.
5. Pray 10 Hail Marys, Glory Be, and Ejaculatory Prayer.
6. Announce the second mystery. Pray an Our Father.
7. Pray 10 Hail Marys, Glory Be, and Ejaculatory Prayer.
8. Announce the third mystery. Pray an Our Father.
9. Pray 10 Hail Marys, Glory Be, and Ejaculatory Prayer.
10. Announce the fourth mystery. Pray an Our Father.
11. Pray 10 Hail Marys, Glory Be, and Ejaculatory Prayer.
12. Announce the fifth mystery. Pray an Our Father.
13. Pray 10 Hail Marys, Glory Be, and Ejaculatory Prayer.
14. Recite the Salve.

Rosary Prayers

Sign of the Cross

"By the sign of the Holy Cross, deliver us from our enemies, O Lord our God. In the name of the Father, and of the Son, and of the Holy Spirit. Amen."

"Santísima Muerte, praised be you, invisible and visible heavenly protector, for the love of God the Father, protect us from all evil."

Apostles' Creed

"I believe in God, the Almighty Father, Creator of Heaven and Earth, and in Jesus Christ, His only son, our Lord who was conceived by the power of the Holy Spirit and born of the Virgin Mary, suffered under Pontius Pilate, was crucified, died, and was buried. He descended into hell. On the third day, he rose again from the dead. He ascended into heaven and is seated at the right hand of God, the Almighty Father. From there, he must come to judge the living and the dead. I believe in the Holy Spirit, the Holy Catholic Church, the Communion of Saints, the forgiveness of sins, the resurrection of the body, and eternal life. Amen."

"Santísima Muerte, praised be you, invisible and visible heavenly protector, because following the omnipotent example of mercy of the one who is one with God, you lavish us with all kinds of care."

Act of Contrition

"My Lord Jesus Christ. True God and true Lord, my Creator, Father and Redeemer, because you are who you are, infinite goodness, and because I love you above all things, it weighs on my heart to have offended you. It also weighs on me because you can punish me with the penalties of hell. With the help of your divine grace, I firmly resolve never to sin again, to confess and to fulfill the penance that will be imposed on me. Amen."

"Santa Muerte, praised be you, invisible and visible heavenly protector, because you fight to prevent suffering to humanity as well as the misfortunes that we might deserve for our own actions."

Our father

"Our Father who art in Heaven, hallowed be thy name. Let your kingdom come. Thy will be done on Earth as it is in Heaven. Give us today our daily bread. Forgive us our sins as we forgive those who sin against us. Lead us not into temptation, and deliver us from evil. Amen."

"Santísima Muerte, praised be you, invisible and visible heavenly protector, because you fight without rest for our salvation."

Hail Mary

"Hail, Mary, full of grace. The Lord is with you. Blessed are you amongst women, and blessed is the fruit of your womb, Jesus. Holy Mary, mother of God, pray for us sinners, now and at the hour of our death. Amen."

"Santa Muerte, praised be you, invisible and visible heavenly protector, for you can enjoy the omnipotence of the Creator's presence, and yet you return to help and protect your less evolved children."

Glory Be

"Glory be to the Father, Glory be to the Son, and Glory be to the Holy Spirit. As it was in the beginning, now and forever and ever and ever. Amen."

"Santísima Muerte, praised be you, invisible and visible heavenly protector, because you suffer the consequences of the sins of humanity for the love of God, mitigating the pain of having committed them."

Ejaculatory Prayers

"Mary, mother of grace, mother of mercy, defend us from our enemies and protect us now and at the hour of our death. Amen."

"O Jesus, forgive us our sins, save us from the fires of Hell and guide all souls to Heaven, especially those who are most in need of your mercy."

"Santa Muerte, praised be you, invisible and visible heavenly protector, because God the Father has granted you the grace to watch over souls and bodies."

Hail

"Hail, Holy Queen, and Mother of Mercy. Our life, our sweetness, and our hope. Hail. To thee do we cry, the exiled children of Eve. To thee do we sigh, mourning and weeping in this valley of tears. Hail, then, O Lady, our advocate. Turn to us those merciful eyes of yours; and after this exile, show us Jesus, blessed fruit of your womb. O clement, O merciful, O ever sweet Virgin Mary!

Pray for us, Holy Mother of God, that we may be worthy to attain the promises of our Lord Jesus Christ. Amen."

Prayer

"Almighty and everlasting God, who, with the cooperation of the Holy Spirit, prepared the body and soul of the glorious Virgin and Mother Mary to be worthy of the dwelling place of your Son. Grant us that, as we celebrate with joy her commemoration through her pious intercession, we may be freed from present evils and eternal death. Through Christ our Lord himself. Amen".

"Santa Muerte, praised be you, heavenly invisible and visible protector, because you save us by suffering our pain: from the earthly hell."

The New Traditional Mysteries (1)

Joyful Mysteries

(Monday and Thursday)

1. The Incarnation of the Son of God.
2. The Visitation of Our Lady to St. Elizabeth.
3. The Birth of the Son of God.
4. The Purification of the Blessed Virgin.
5. The Loss of the Child Jesus and His finding in the Temple.

Sorrowful Mysteries

(Tuesday and Friday)

1. The Prayer of Our Lord in the Garden.
2. The Flagellation of the Lord.
3. The Crowning with Thorns.
4. The Way of Mount Calvary.
5. The Crucifixion and Death of Our Lord.

Glorious Mysteries

(Wednesday, Saturday, and Sunday)

1. The Resurrection of the Lord.
2. The Ascension of the Lord.
3. The Coming of the Holy Spirit.
4. The Assumption of Our Lady into Heaven.
5. The Coronation of the Blessed Virgin.

Luminous Mysteries

(Thursday)

1. The Baptism of Jesus in the Jordan.
2. Jesus' self-revelation at the Wedding at Cana.
3. The Announcement of the Kingdom of God, inviting Conversion.
4. The Transfiguration.
5. The Institution of the Eucharist.

(1) In the Apostolic Letter "Rosarium Virginis Mariae" (2002), John Paul II proposes for the contemplation of believers the new Mysteries

of Light or Luminous Mysteries, so-called because in his public life, Christ manifests himself as a Mystery of Light: "While I am in the world, I am the light of the world." These new Mysteries are prayed on Thursdays, passing the second contemplation of the Joyful Mysteries to Saturday.

Invocation and farewell to Santa Muerte

God Almighty Father, Creator of Heaven and Earth, of all things visible and invisible. Lord, we ask your permission to invoke the Santa Muerte, My White Child, My Marvelous Rose.

Invocation to Holy Death

"Santísima Muerte, Santísima Muerte, Santísima Muerte. We ask you to come to us and join in the joy that we feel when we are with you, my White Child. My Marvelous Rose, guide us along the way and protect us from all evil."

"Santísima Muerte, Santísima Muerte, Santísima Muerte. Come, Our Lady. We ask to venerate you and let us feel you. Fill us with joy, since you give protection by being with us. We fear nothing because we will be able to overcome all obstacles with the virtues that you possess. Santa Muerte of Our Heart, do not abandon us and give us your protection."

"Santísima Muerte, come to us, we ask you from our heart. Thank you, thank you, thank you, Santísima Muerte, for being with us. In the name of God, Almighty Father, we offer you and pray the following novena of prayers. Thank you, White Child. Thank you, Marvelous Rose, for your presence with us. Blessed you for listening to us."

"We thank you for the protection that you give us and we ask you to come every time that we or someone who needs you, invokes you. My White Child, we thank you. Blessed are you, Santa Muerte, thank you for granting us this great time of joy."

THANK YOU, Santa Muerte!

THANK YOU, MARVELOUS ROSE!

THANK YOU, WHITE CHILD!

Novena of Fire to the Santa Muerte

FIRST DAY

Transmutation

Powerful messenger of God, here I come to lay at your feet all that is negativity in my life.

In front of you I leave the spirits that I do not want to see walking around the corners of my house: envy, resentment, jealousy, despair, lacking, and all their brothers who are similar to them.

But above all, here I leave you the spirit of fear that hurts me so much.

Take them please. I do not need them. All they do is confuse my thoughts and upset my emotions.

Recycle them. Transmute them. Bring in the spirits of peace, wisdom, trust, hope, and prosperity consciousness instead.

Send to me the spirit of courage and tell him that I want to see him arrive hand in hand with the spirit of love.

Here I await your reply with a trusting heart.

SECOND DAY

Forgiveness

Dear White Girl: Before you I bring all my grudges. Those rancors that at times turn into hatred and that circulate through my mind repeating over and over again scenes of retribution and revenge.

Those thoughts where I see myself as a victim, expose me to attract victimizers and disadvantaged situations into my life.

I know and despite that, it is difficult for me to let go of these grievances.

That's why, White Girl, I leave them here at your feet so you can help me let go of the feelings of being betrayed or defeated.

Help me to forgive, not because my offenders deserve it, but because I deserve to live in peace.

I deserve to have thoughts of being a conqueror. I deserve to attract situations where I come out on top. I deserve to have a free mind and a serene spirit.

Here I await your reply with a trusting heart.

THIRD DAY

Health

Beautiful White Death: On this day I give you my body, my mind, and my spirit. The three levels of which I am composed.

They all need repair. Enter the cells of my body and help them to function in harmony: clean, healthy, punctual and perfect.

In my mind, blow fresh winds that take away that voice that scolds me because it thinks I'm not a perfect being. Also cleanse me of thoughts of defeat and fear. Let clear, happy, optimistic and helpful thoughts flow through my mind.

Of my spirit, what can I tell you? You know it better than anyone. Please heal all the burdens that my ancestors left on me. Cleanse me of karmas that may have existed long before my body was conceived. Let my spirit float free and sovereign, purified and full of love.

Here I await your reply with a trusting heart.

FOURTH DAY

Truth

Santísima Muerte, come now and bring with you the truth. I want to see her walk powerful, relentless and accurate. May she be the one to open the windows so that the light enters my conscience.

I want her to manifest now. It doesn't matter if I don't like what she has to say. I prefer to know what I need to know because I know that after I face my truth, I will find the peace that has so eluded me until now.

Bring her.

Let me see her.

Tell the truth that she must speak clearly to me, that she doesn't have to sugarcoat her words, that my heart is ready to listen to her.

Because I know that only then can I be free again.

Here I await your reply with a trusting heart. Amen.

FIFTH DAY

Justice

Santa Muerte, you who carry the scale with you, I ask you today with humility, to weigh well in each side of your scale the truths that you have witnessed.

You well know that in all trials each one expresses their truth so that you, divine justice, determine who wins and who loses in the destinies of life.

I will see you, with my calm heart, exercise your role as judge on the issues that hang over my life.

I will calmly accept your verdict. I will accept it knowing that the justice you mete out is implacable.

And if you decide against me, I understand that it will be because you have information that I cannot see from my human perspective.

I accept it and I thank you, because I know that when you close a door on me, you always open new paths for me, always just, always wise. And that something better will await me after that.

And if I win because you have seen my truth and decided to rule in my favor, from the bottom of my hear, I give you thanks.

Here I await your reply with a trusting heart. Amen.

SIXTH DAY

Protection

Holy Death that always walks by my side and protects me at all times, today I come to thank you for my safety and that of my family.

Thank you that you protect our bodies from all visible or invisible danger. From sunrise to sunset and from when the sun goes down until the sun comes up again. From south to north and from east to west.

Thank you because you protect our minds and fill them with hope and with strength.

Thank you because you protect our spirits and teach us to sow hope and good future in the spiritual plane.

Thank you, my Saint, because your protection reaches us at all times. Keep doing it, we need it today more than yesterday.

Here I await your reply with a trusting heart. Amen.

SEVENTH DAY

Prosperity

My dear and much appreciated Santa Muerte: Every morning that I leave my house I always ask you to help me put food on the table, roof over our heads and money in our wallets.

And you always deliver. Thank you. Thank you. Thank you. Today I humbly ask you to continue to prosper me. That you allow me to continue paying my bills on time and that there is always money in my wallet to help whoever you send my way and that I can help.

I also ask you to help me save a little to protect my family from any eventuality.

I ask you to allow money to flow constantly, healthy, perfect and clean to my wallet, to my bank and whenever I need it. I promise to make good use of what you send me.

I await your reply with a trusting heart. Amen

EIGHTH DAY

Power

Holy Death of my heart: here I come to your feet to ask you to fill me with power.

Of that power of yours that knows no borders, that does not accept defeat, that even if I should fall, I will get up again to continue fighting.

I want my body, my mind and my spirit to be filled with your power. May you instill in me that encouragement that makes me move forward towards my goals.

That I know how to protect my people and my possessions, with integrity, and with a cold mind and a tireless body.

Let nothing stop me, except reason and truth, so that full of wisdom and courage, I persist along the paths of light until I see my goals of good and justice, respect and prosperity; nobility and dedication to the service of those who depend on me, all properly fulfilled.

Here I await your reply with a trusting heart. Amen.

NINTH DAY

Love

Holy Death please fill me with love. Make my heart and my senses fill with that love that seeks to serve, protect and make life easier for the beings we love. Pour over me a rain of that love that envelops, that transforms and that is always willing to give a little more of itself.

For the love of a couple, if I don't have it, I ask you to send it to me. If I already I have, I ask you to strengthen it.

For the love of my elders and my children, I ask you to fill it with respect and patience so that I can serve and support them in the years to come every time and every where they need me.

For the love of my friends, I ask you to fill it with loyalty. Let them know that they can trust me and that I'll stand by them whenever they need me.

For the love of others, I ask you to leave compassion in my senses so that I stop when I see others suffer and with generosity and a good spirit of service, I reach out to them in your name.

For the love of my own person, I ask you to enlighten me so that I learn to see my good side and respect myself; to take care of myself as I deserve and to talk to myself about positive matters that move me towards a plane of peace and joy for being who I am without wanting to be anybody else.

Here I await your reply with a trusting heart. Amen.

INDEX

PRAYERS

© First Edition in Spanish, Guerrero Editores, México 1995
© **1st Edition in Spanish USA Calli Casa Editorial 2014**
2a Edition in Spanish, revised, USA, Calli Casa Editorial 2021
1st. Edition in English, USA, Yhacar Trust, 2022

General Supervision: Bernabé Pérez
Cover Illustration: Mehmet Can Doğan (fiverr.com/mecandon)
www.2GoodLuck.com
jbooks909@gmail.com, Lake Elsinore, CA 92530

Made in the USA
Middletown, DE
22 December 2023

46680644R00053